WHOLE WIDE WORLD
TAJ MAHAL

by Kristine Spanier, MLIS

Ideas for Parents and Teachers

Pogo Books let children practice reading informational text while introducing them to nonfiction features such as headings, labels, sidebars, maps, and diagrams, as well as a table of contents, glossary, and index.

Carefully leveled text with a strong photo match offers early fluent readers the support they need to succeed.

Before Reading

- "Walk" through the book and point out the various nonfiction features. Ask the student what purpose each feature serves.
- Look at the glossary together. Read and discuss the words.

Read the Book

- Have the child read the book independently.
- Invite him or her to list questions that arise from reading.

After Reading

- Discuss the child's questions. Talk about how he or she might find answers to those questions.
- Prompt the child to think more. Ask: Did you know about the Taj Mahal before you read this book? What more would you like to learn?

Pogo Books are published by Jump!
5357 Penn Avenue South
Minneapolis, MN 55419
www.jumplibrary.com

Library of Congress Cataloging-in-Publication Data

Names: Spanier, Kristine, author.
Title: Taj Mahal / by Kristine Spanier.
Description: Minneapolis, MN: Jump!, Inc., [2021]
Series: Whole wide World | Includes index.
Audience: Ages 7-10 | Audience: Grades 2-3
Identifiers: LCCN 2020030780 (print)
LCCN 2020030781 (ebook)
ISBN 9781645277507 (hardcover)
ISBN 9781645277514 (paperback)
ISBN 9781645277521 (ebook)
Subjects: LCSH: Taj Mahal (Agra, India)—Juvenile literature.
Mausoleums—India—Agra—Juvenile literature.
Agra (India)—Buildings, structures, etc. –Juvenile literature.
Classification: LCC DS486.A3 S68 2021 (print)
LCC DS486.A3 (ebook) | DDC 954/.2–dc23
LC record available at https://lccn.loc.gov/2020030780
LC ebook record available at https://lccn.loc.gov/2020030781

Editor: Jenna Gleisner
Designer: Molly Ballanger

Photo Credits: turtix/Shutterstock, cover; Mikadun/Shutterstock, 1; StockImageFactory.com/Shutterstock, 3; Dinodia Photos/Alamy, 4; Cat Downie/Shutterstock, 5; Yosanon Y/Shutterstock, 6-7; Abdallah Ahmad Maqboul/Shutterstock, 8; Daily Travel Photos/Shutterstock, 9; mammuth/iStock, 10-11; Tim Graham/robertharding/SuperStock, 12-13; Yakov Oskanov/Shutterstock, 14-15; unununius photo/Shutterstock, 16-17; Martina Badini/Shutterstock, 18; Alamy, 19; Meinzahn/iStock, 20-21; Tanarch/Shutterstock, 23.

Printed in the United States of America at Corporate Graphics in North Mankato, Minnesota.

TABLE OF CONTENTS

CHAPTER 1

THE QUEEN'S TOMB

Mumtaz Mahal was queen of the Mughal **Empire**. It was in India. She died in 1631. Her husband was **Emperor** Shah Jahan. He wanted to **honor** her.

Mumtaz Mahal

Shah Jahan

The Taj Mahal was built for the queen's **tomb**. The name means "Crown of Palaces." It is in Agra, India, next to the Yamuna River. It took around 20 years to build and decorate. More than 20,000 workers helped.

Yamuna River

Four main buildings and a garden make up the **complex**. Near the river is the **mausoleum**. This was built to hold the tomb.

mausoleum

TAKE A LOOK!

Take a look at a map of the complex. Notice the balanced design.

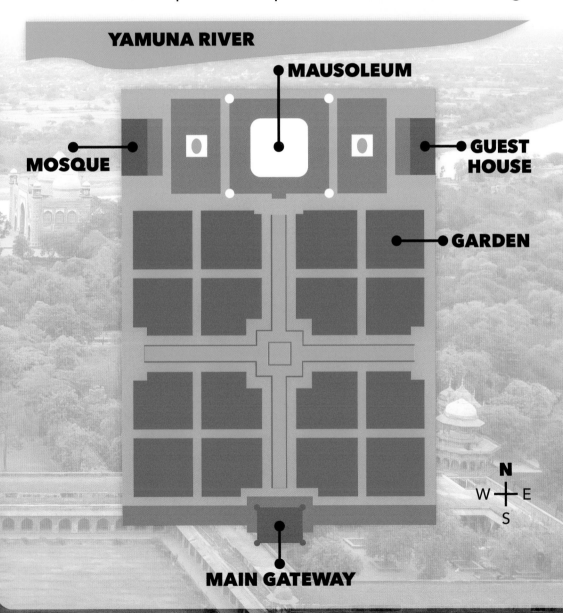

YAMUNA RIVER

MAUSOLEUM

MOSQUE

GUEST HOUSE

GARDEN

MAIN GATEWAY

N
W E
S

CHAPTER 2

A BEAUTIFUL PALACE

The main gateway stands at one end. It is made of red sandstone. The central arch is two stories high.

arch

A long pool of water **reflects** the mausoleum. Trees line walking paths.

The mausoleum is made of white marble. The dome reaches 240 feet (73 meters). Each side of the building is the same. An arch is at each center. **Minarets** stand at each corner. Each one is more than 130 feet (40 m) tall.

DID YOU KNOW?

White marble reflects light. The mausoleum changes color as Earth rotates.

cenotaph

Two cenotaphs are inside the
mausoleum. These are empty
tombs. They honor the emperor
and the queen. Their real tombs
are buried underground.

Two buildings stand at the garden edges. They look the same on the outside. One is a **mosque**. Marble designs on the floor look like prayer rugs. There are 569 of them!

The second building is a guest house. It was used for guests who came to honor the queen.

mosque

Arabic words

mosaic

Floral **mosaics** decorate the buildings. So do Arabic words. What do they say? Some are verses from the Qur'an. This is a **sacred** Muslim book.

WHAT DO YOU THINK?

The words and decorations have special meanings. What if you could decorate a building? What would you show? Why?

CHAPTER 3
THE TAJ MAHAL TODAY

The Taj Mahal is a **symbol** of love. Why? The emperor wanted a place of great beauty for his wife.

People from all around the world come to visit. The mosque closes to tourists for two hours on Fridays. Why? People who live nearby pray inside.

Anyone can visit the palace where the queen is buried. But people have to follow rules to help **preserve** the site. They must take their shoes off to protect the floors. They can only stay for three hours. Would you like to see the Taj Mahal?

WHAT DO YOU THINK?

Pollution is a danger to the site. Some nearby factories have been closed. Cars that use gas are not allowed near it. How do you protect your environment?

QUICK FACTS & TOOLS

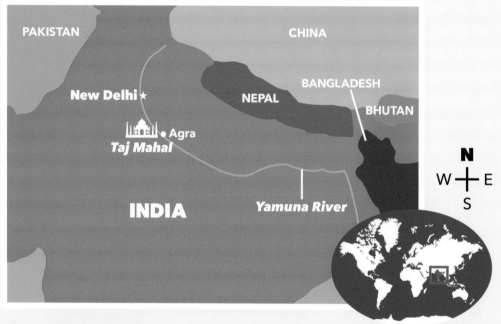

TAJ MAHAL

Location: Agra, India

Size: 42 acres (17 hectares)

Years Built: 1632 to 1648

Primary Architect:
Ustad Ahmad Lahauri

Past Use: mausoleum

Current Use: mausoleum, cultural site, and visitor attraction

Number of Visitors Each Year:
around 6.5 million

GLOSSARY

complex: A group of buildings that are near each other and are used for similar purposes.

emperor: The ruler of an empire.

empire: A group of countries or states that have the same ruler.

honor: To show respect.

mausoleum: A building that contains a tomb or tombs.

minarets: Tall, slim towers of a mosque, from which Muslims are called to prayer.

mosaics: Patterns or pictures made up of small pieces of colored stone, tile, or glass.

mosque: A building where Muslims worship.

preserve: To protect something so that it stays in its original or current state.

reflects: Shows an image of something on a shiny surface.

sacred: Holy or having to do with religion.

symbol: An object that stands for, suggests, or represents something else.

tomb: A grave, room, or building that holds a dead body.

INDEX

TO LEARN MORE

Finding more information is as easy as 1, 2, 3.

① Go to www.factsurfer.com

② Enter "TajMahal" into the search box.

③ Choose your book to see a list of websites.

FACT SURFER